LIFE IN CALIFORNIA: 1930–1950

This catalogue is published in conjunction with the exhibition
Life in California: 1930–1950
September 25, 2008 to January 18, 2009
Organized by the Santa Barbara Historical Museum

© 2008 Santa Barbara Historical Museum
136 East De la Guerra Street, Santa Barbara, CA 93101
Telephone (805) 966-1601 • Fax (805) 966-1603
www.santabarbaramuseum.com

ISBN: 0-9704940-4-1

Front cover:
CHARLES PAYZANT
Early Wilshire Boulevard, 1931

Back cover:
BARSE MILLER, N.A. (1904–1973)
Rainy Day – Fort Mason, 1943

vi
Photograph
Wilshire Boulevard, 1932
SECURITY PACIFIC COLLECTION / Los Angeles Public Library.

LIFE IN CALIFORNIA: 1930–1950

SCENE PAINTINGS FROM THE SALLY AND DAVID MARTIN COLLECTION

SANTA BARBARA HISTORICAL MUSEUM

CONTENTS

FOREWORD

David S. Bisol, Executive Director, Santa Barbara Historical Museum

Life in California, 1930–1950 is another milestone for the Santa Barbara Historical Museum: this is our first exhibition devoted solely to works from one local private art collection, and the first to present art representing so much of California, from Ft. Bragg in the north to San Diego in the south.

The focus of this museum is, properly, on our local history, which is illustrated in this institution's signature exhibition, *The Story of Santa Barbara*. But Santa Barbara does not exist in a geographical vacuum any more than one time period can be entirely separated from earlier, or later, years. So it is fitting that we broaden our horizons to embrace and examine what our state was like during several pivotal periods in California's history: the Great Depression, World War II and the immediate post-war years.

The watercolors and oils included in this exhibition show us, vividly and dramatically, what these times were all about. They also give us a wonderful opportunity to appreciate the inventiveness of a group of uniquely progressive Californian artists.

I am extremely grateful to Historical Museum Trustee Marlene R. Miller for contributing her professional expertise as Guest Curator of this exhibition. Her willingness to volunteer the time, energy and talent needed to oversee all aspects of its presentation is an inspiration to us all, and represents an invaluable element of support for this Museum's mission: ensuring history always plays an important role in all of our lives.

I would also like to thank Nancy Dustin Wall Moure for writing her scholarly essay, *Scenes of California Life*, for this catalogue and extend my personal thanks to Douglas A. Diller, Assistant Director/Curator, for the exhibition's superb installation, and to Michael Redmon, Director of Research and former Museum Trustee, Warren Miller for their editing expertise.

But it is my special privilege to extend to Sally and David Martin the profound gratitude of the entire Historical Museum community for entrusting us with these artistic treasures from their personal collection. In addition to giving us the opportunity to enjoy these interpretations of mid-20th Century California, the Martins' generosity highlights another facet of our unique community, the ability and vision of special people to preserve a body of work that is valued as much for its historical importance as for its artistic merit.

Sally and David Martin

INTRODUCTION

Marlene R. Miller, Guest Curator

Sally and David Martin began collecting California Scene paintings in 1988, after seeing *Regionalism: The California View* exhibition at the Santa Barbara Museum of Art. For these Santa Barbara residents there was an instant connection with the time period, the locales and the painting style. They appreciated the unique qualities of these artists who were able to understand, and capture with exuberance, the area where they lived and worked.

This group of artists, variously named California Scene Painters, The California Group, The California School and California Regionalists, are an extension of the American Scene or American Regionalist movement. Rex Brandt, one of the most influential participants in and teachers of the California movement, summed it up this way:

In barely one hundred years, the artist's view of his surroundings underwent great changes, shifting from heroic cartographic views of unpeopled vastness, painted in the brownish chiaroscuro style imported from the nineteenth-century academics of Munich and Dusseldorf, to the genial atmospheric canvases of the impressionists and luminists. This, the plein air view, was to dominate the salons of San Francisco and Los Angeles through the 1920s. Then, with the advent of the Depression, it lost its audience. The stage was set for another step.

The next generation turned to the ancillary arts for a means of survival. With no sense of frustration, they moved into mural painting, motion picture set design, animation, illustration, teaching and design—everything from advertisements to housing projects.... The works have a muscular, virile and organic quality that transcends the often commonplace subject matter. At best, there is a presence celebrating the fact of being alive and vividly aware of the world. *

American Scene paintings of everyday activities were the new subjects: artwork that was uniquely American. The California Group began with the formation of the California Water Color Society, which was founded in Los Angeles in 1920. Although the founders were primarily painters in oil, they realized that watercolors were ideally suited to convey the delicate nuances of the California light. And even though these artists had similar artistic education and training, they developed an incredible range of style, use of color and imagination. Each artist found his own means of expression for depicting—indeed, telling stories about—life in California: the everyday life in the developing cities, farming in the rural countryside, industrial sites, people working or just having fun. This relatively small group of friends enjoyed the camaraderie of painting, traveling and exhibiting together while recording the world around them. The narrative quality of these paintings is also a reflection of the fact that, during the Depression, many of the artists worked as illustrators and animators

---

* Ruth Lilly Westphal and Janet Blake Dominick, *American Scene Painting: California, 1930s and 1940s* (Irvine, CA: Westphal Publishing, 1991), 11.

3

for Walt Disney and other movie studios that were producing animated films.

All of the artists in this exhibition were members of the California Water Color Society, which became the National Watercolor Society in 1975. After Millard Sheets, Phil Dike, Lee Blair, Barse Miller, Phil Paradise, James Patrick and Hardy Gramatky joined the Society in the late 1920s, a definable style evolved. Millard Sheets, who taught watercolor painting to many of the California School artists at the Chouinard Art Institute, was the driving force behind the movement. Rex Brandt, Emil Kosa Jr., Dan Lutz, Tom Craig, George Post, Mary Blair and Milford Zornes soon joined the group. By 1948 the membership had grown to more than 250 members. Some of the artists, including Dong Kingman and George Post, lived and worked in the San Francisco Bay Area, recording life in that region.

In the late 1930s the representational style of watercolor painting was at its zenith. Artists were invited to exhibit their paintings in the East, some were represented in prestigious galleries throughout the country, and national magazines would feature West Coast artists on a regular basis. In 1940 the California Water Color Society invited eleven Eastern artists to their annual exhibition. Among them were Reginald March, Charles Burchfield and Andrew Wyeth. It was hailed as the finest regional show of contemporary watercolors in the world. This notoriety got the attention of *Life* magazine, which featured works by Brandt, Dike, Kingman, Kosa, Miller and Patrick in an October 1941 issue.

With the onset of World War II, people's interests were more directed towards defense, international affairs and patriotic matters. The Army selected forty-two artists to work overseas, among them Standish Backus, Jr., Edward Reep and Milford Zornes; Barse Miller served as chief of the Combat Art Section in the Pacific Theater. All three major services—Army, Navy and Marine Corps—recognized the importance of art to record the war experience for the American people. All of those involved were soldiers and sailors first and artists only when time permitted, but they created an important body of work that proved very useful in rallying public support for the war effort. In addition to the uniformed artists, a number of others, including Tom Craig and Barse Miller, experienced the war firsthand as artist-correspondents for *Life* magazine.

During the postwar years, The California School began to change rapidly. Many newly educated artists were creating abstract works and the public became increasingly interested in that genre. Some artists of the original group, including Sheets, Dike and Brandt, had been experimenting with abstraction for a number of years, but without public acceptance. Though these artists continued to explore new styles, others, including Kosa, Payzant and Backus, remained faithful to their representational traditions. So did Milford Zornes, whose death at age 100 finally ended his remarkable career as both painter and teacher.

Through these artists' works we have an opportunity to revisit California as it was during a time in our state's history that many of us experienced firsthand, but that our children and grandchildren must learn about from historical imagery such as these paintings. Thanks to dedicated collectors such as Sally and David Martin, we have that important opportunity.

SCENES OF CALIFORNIA LIFE, 1930–1950

Nancy Dustin Wall Moure

Between 1930 and 1950, a movement called American Scene Painting, which depicted the American landscape and its people, arose in reaction to earlier popular European-inspired styles such as Impressionism, Cubism, Futurism and Fauvism that most American painters espoused between 1890 and 1920. New York/Midwest artist Thomas Hart Benton is looked upon as the first to combine sensual shapes and lines with scenes of American life to create this new movement.

Through the 1920s the movement gained popularity and spread outside New York City, then the center of American art. Wanting to keep abreast of the times, California artists, who learned of the style through national art magazines and by traveling to New York, adopted it. American artists were further encouraged to use their own country as subject matter when the tight financial conditions of the Depression prevented many from making the European grand tour, *de rigueur* for earlier painters. After 1933, government-sponsored art projects, meant to help relieve artists' poverty, went so far as to prescribe American Scene themes.

As opposed to the elitist subject matter of Impressionism, American Scene was democratic, and focused on rural landscapes and the lifestyle of the average American. With artists of each state receiving approbation for depictions of their regions' idiosyncrasies, for the first time in American history the art leadership of New York and the Northeast was challenged.

Art historian Matthew Baigell defined two main categories of American Scene: Regionalist and Social Realist. Regionalist works depict landscapes or people engaged in pleasant everyday activities such as family gatherings, manual work and attending entertainments such as the circus. Most California artists preferred this kind of subject matter, which proclaimed the basic goodness of America in spite of hard financial times.

Social Realist works, on the other hand, are critical of America's shortcomings and depict subjects such as labor strikes, hoboes, the lifestyle of the very poor, and human tragedy. Such scenes were less common in California than elsewhere in the country, and only a few California Scene artists painted Social Realist themes.

Artists did not belong to these groups; rather, the subject matter of individual works placed them in these categories retrospectively for the purpose of art historical analysis.

CALIFORNIA WITHIN THE AMERICAN SCENE

Although California was physically and psychologically far from New York, artists here did not hesitate long before adopting American Scene subject matter. By the late 1920s, California had the second largest population of artists after New York.

Watercolor was the preferred medium of California Scene painters. Watercolor as a valid medium for fine art emerged in late 1700s England. Through the 1800s, the delicate and timid medium usually rendered detailed landscapes. Near the end of the century, American artists such as Winslow Homer began to paint with bolder color and brushwork and eliminate detail. This trend was advanced in the late 1920s when a number of California artists, who studied at the Chouinard Art Institute in Los Angeles, became very bold and expressive with the medium. Not restricted by East Coast conservatism, they were open-minded toward experimentation, wanted to realize a scene quickly, and willingly shared technical discoveries with painter friends. Their style is now termed the "California Style" and is identified by large-sized papers, bold and broad brushwork, and strong colors.

California Scene painters preferred watercolor to oil, as it was quicker to work with and could spontaneously capture fleeting incidents they observed. (Some did, however, also paint in oil.) They used watercolor to depict both landscapes and genre paintings. California geography and terrain, as well as the look of her cities and the activities of her people, provided unique subject matter compared to other states, and depictions of it made a genuine contribution to the national movement. Inspired by the enthusiasm of their unofficial leader, Millard Sheets, many Los Angeles-based artists roamed their city and seized any curious and picturesque subject that came within their view. Opportunistic and executed on the spot, watercolors were truer reflections of California life than some oils which tried to force the California genre into national themes. Watercolors were conservative in subject matter, however, and most fell into the category of Regionalism.

LIFE IN THE DEPRESSION

Today, because of images left to us by dramatic newsreel footage, motion pictures and still photographs, the term Great Depression conjures up labor strikes, hobos, bread lines and ruined dustbowl farms.

However most Americans, particularly semi-rural Californians, suffered fewer hardships than the strike-torn Northeast or the drought-ravaged Midwest and Great Plains states. While money was not plentiful, those who led financially conservative lives were generally able to ride out the bad years without too much deprivation. California artists survived by taking paying jobs as art teachers or working for the motion picture studios, or as decorators, designers or draftsmen.

Many artists also qualified for the public works art projects initiated during the Depression. Beginning in 1933 the federal government sponsored a number of programs to employ out-of-work artists to create murals for a wide variety of public buildings, posters and paintings. More than 5,000 artists were employed in these public works programs, creating more than 200,000 works of art for the American people. These programs lasted until 1943, by which time the economic stimulus of war production had made most of the New Deal economic support programs unnecessary.

CALIFORNIA SCENE SUBJECTS

Landscape prevailed as California Scene painters' favorite subjects. California is one of the most geographically varied states, with its dramatic coastlines, rolling farmland, deserts and snow-capped mountains. Not ravaged by drought, the state's landscape was a positive subject, confirming its scenic beauty as well as its economic potential.

Southern and Northern California artists were attracted to different areas of the state, possibly influenced by the few roads that existed and the scarcity of both private vehicles and fuel. Southern Californians traveled to rural areas within a few hours' drive of her major cities of San Diego, Los Angeles and Santa Barbara. They also followed Route 101 north along the coast and Route 395 up the dry eastern side of the Sierras.

Northern California artists restricted their travels to San Francisco Bay, to Monterey, and to the farming areas of Salinas and the Carmel Valley. Some, like Thomas Craig in his *Gold Hill*, painted the former gold mining towns of the Sierra Nevada. These abandoned shafts and towns symbolized America's destruction in the Depression.

Gold Hill, undated

Artists from both north and south depicted the eastern deserts. The hardy plants struggling in an inhospitable environment symbolized the American people struggling against the hardships of the Depression. California artists even traveled to Taos, New Mexico and to Mexico where they found picturesque Native American and Indio subject matter, both groups representative of the world's poorer populations.

Farmscapes were one of the most popular subjects. In American Scene thinking, a healthy and productive farm symbolized America's true strength, a solid asset. California in the 1930s offered many subjects, since much of the state was relegated to farming. Farms ranged from dry wheat farming to cattle and sheep ranching, small truck farms, dairy farms, and orange groves and vineyards. Most farm paintings were long-distance views showing farm buildings set amid rolling hills, sometimes with horses in pastures. Milford Zornes' *Cerro Romualdo* is an example. When labor was represented, it was manual, not mechanized: the big mechanized and commercial farms of the flat San Joaquin Valley held little interest. The national icon of a farmer plowing with horses was replaced in California with bean pickers, fruit and walnut gatherers, and carrot bundlers. Phil Dike's *Smudging* heroicizes workers hurrying to light smudge pots whose rising heat will circulate air through the orange grove and keep the fruit from freezing.

The second most popular landscape subject revolved around California's coastline. As artists depict what they see, San Francisco artists portrayed activities around their great bay, including its marshes, fishing boats, ocean liners, ferries and stevedores. Examples are George Post's *San Francisco Waterfront* and Standish Backus's *Camp by the Sea*. They also painted Monterey's fishing industry. The warmer weather in Southern California, as well as the location of several summer watercolor schools in Laguna Beach, Corona del Mar and Newport Harbor, led her artists to depict the shore's recreational activities such as sunbathing and yachting, as in Phil Dike's *Harbor Life*. San Diego artists painted the activities of the 11th Naval District's officers and enlisted men.

Cityscapes, formerly popular with New York artists but anathema to Californians, grew in popularity. Los Angeles artists, many encouraged to the subject by watercolorist and teacher Millard Sheets, roamed downtown on the lookout for interesting architectural subjects and tenements, as did Joseph Weisman, who found his *Purple Duck Cafe* and ethnic neighborhoods like Olvera Street. San Francisco artists, more city-bound than Southern California artists and surrounded by more picturesque subjects, depicted their city's Victorian houses, Chinatown, its docks and, after 1936, the two great bridges. See Dong Kingman's *San Francisco*, in which the city seems blessed with a ray of light.

Industrial themes were popular on a national level, as factories and big industry were associated with the triumph of science and engineering as well as with the drudgery of hourly work and the struggle of organized labor. Before World War II California had relatively few industrial areas. In Northern California shipbuilding went on in Richmond and Oakland, and in Southern California there were quarries, the new motion picture industry and the harbors. Most artists painted overall views of factory complexes, delighting in their pipes, towers and tanks rather than depicting individual people at work, as did Emil Kosa in his *San Pedro Harbor*. Thomas Craig's *Mill at Fort Bragg* with its dark colors and polluting smoke speaks against industrialization.

Vehicles were also a favorite subject. The automobile, which first became generally available in the 1920s, was an emblem of luxury; it symbolized mobility and freedom and power. But in its ruined state the auto symbolized America's destroyed economy. Ironically, although cars are most identified with Los Angeles, it was the Berkeley artist John Haley and his followers who found such things as gas stations and road signs worthy subjects. Trains were also associated with mobility and freedom; their whistles were haunting, and they provided transportation for hobos. San Franciscans also depicted cable cars, as did Lee Blair. Heavy equipment, such as Dan Lutz's *Steam Shovel*, symbolized hardwork.

Steam Shovel, 1937

Genre paintings, or views of people at work or play, were fewer in number but could be set against any of the above backdrops. Because California had fewer social troubles, its artists could neither relate to nor experience things like starvation, ruined cropland, or industrial strikes. Most genre scenes are therefore upbeat, even with a sense of humor, as Californians are depicted going about their everyday activities. Very often these were recreational, as in Charles Payzant's *The Ball Players*. Genre scenes of negative subjects were rarely painted, and then mostly by San Francisco artists caught up with intellectual concerns and influenced by the Mexican pro-Communist muralist Diego Rivera, who worked in the town briefly. Some San Francisco artists depicted the dock strikes in which many laborers were killed.

CALIFORNIA SCENE DURING WORLD WAR II

By the late 1930s, the American Scene movement had run its course. With the advent of World War II, the deprivations of Americans and Californians seemed minor in view of the suffering in Europe and Asia.

Artists of the California Style continued painting watercolors and depicting the local scene, some of it military, although Americans were warned against making photographic or other depictions of sensitive coastal military installations, as the images might fall into enemy hands. Phil Paradise depicts four views of Red Cross work. A significant number of California watercolorists were hired both by the government and by national magazines, such as *Life*, to paint war scenes, and were sent to the various theaters of war in Europe, North Africa, Southeast Asia and India. Most did not pursue the propagandistic role of earlier war painters like Arthur Beaumont who painted powerful images of naval ships. Instead they showed the average service-man as he went about his duties or spent time on leave, as Rex Brandt did in his *Horsemen at Mission Beach*, which shows U. S. Navy sailors riding a merry-go-round.

POST WAR CALIFORNIA SCENE

Artists who began their careers in the late 1920s and were comfortable with California Scene subject matter and the watercolor medium, continued it to their deaths with few changes. Some absorbed the angular and flat tendencies of post-war abstraction, and their subject matter featured new aspects of California life such as freeways, life in house trailers, and drive-in restaurants. Herbert Ryman's MGM *Marina* depicts a spot on MGM Studio's back lot.

California Scene watercolorists and oil painters have left a rich picture of life between 1930 and 1950. Their views allow us an intimate look back at this seemingly innocent period. It's nostalgia perhaps, but California Scene paintings actually present a truer picture of life during that era, emphasizing people's humanity and humility, than the better-known and more sensational news and motion picture reportage that generally focused on negative spectacular events.

ABOUT THE AUTHOR

Nancy Moure is a freelance curator and writer specializing in the field of historic California art. She obtained her M.A. in art history from UCLA and was Assistant Curator of American Art at the Los Angeles County Museum of Art for fifteen years. Her *Dictionary of Art and Artists in Southern California Before 1930*, first issued in 1975, was a pioneering work in the field of California art history. She has followed this up with more than fifty books and articles, and in 1998 completed *California Art: 450 Years of Painting and Other Media*, the first tome to survey the state's art from its beginnings to the present. This essay is a revision of one that appeared in *Scenes of California Life, 1930–1950*, published in 1991 by The Dorian Society, California State University, Bakersfield to accompany an exhibition of the same name at the University's Todd Madigan Gallery.

FURTHER READING

Anderson, Susan M. *Regionalism: The California View, Watercolors, 1929-1945*. Santa Barbara: Santa Barbara Museum of Art, 1988.

Baigell, Matthew. *The American Scene: American Painting of the 1930s*. New York: Praeger Publishers, 1974.

Dominik, Janet B. *California School: From the Private Collection of E. Gene Crain*. Gualala, CA: Gualala Arts, 1986.

Hughes, Edan Milton. *Artists in California: 1786-1940*. 2d ed. San Francisco: Hughes Publishing Company, 1989.

Kingman, Helena Kuo, and Dong Kingman. *Dong Kingman's Watercolors*. New York: Watson-Guptill Publications, 1980.

Laguna Beach Museum of Art. *Millard Sheets: Six Decades of Painting*. Laguna Beach, CA: Laguna Beach Museum of Art, 1983.

Lovoos, Janice. *Two from California: Joan Irving, Rex Brandt*. Riverside, CA: The Riverside Art Center and Museum, 1984.

Lovoos, Janice, and Edmund F. Penney. *Millard Sheets: One-Man Renaissance*. Flagstaff, AZ: Northland Press, 1984.

Lovoos, Janice, and Gordon T. McClelland. *Phil Dike*. Beverly Hills, CA: Hillcrest Press, Inc., 1988.

McClelland, Gordon T. *Emil Kosa, Jr.* Beverly Hills, CA: Hillcrest Press, Inc., 1990.

_____. *George Post*. Beverly Hills, CA: Hillcrest Press, Inc. 1991.

McClelland, Gordon T., and Jay T. Last. *California Watercolors, 1850-1970*. Santa Ana, CA: Hillcrest Press, Inc., 2002.

_____. *The California Style: California Watercolors, 1925-1955*. Beverly Hills, CA: Hillcrest Press, Inc., 1985.

McClelland, Gordon T., and Milford Zornes. *Milford Zornes*. Beverly Hills, CA: Hillcrest Press, Inc. 1991.

Moure, Nancy Dustin Wall. *Scenes of California Life, 1930-1950*. Bakersfield, CA: The Dorian Society, 1991.

Perine, Robert. *Chouinard: An Art Vision Betrayed*. Encinitas, CA: Artra Publishing, Inc. 1985.

Reep, Ed. *A Combat Artist in World War II*. Lexington, KY: The University Press of Kentucky, 1987.

Westphal, Ruth Lilly, and Janet Blake Dominik, eds. *American Scene Painting: California, 1930s and 1940s*. Irvine, CA: Westphal Publishing. 1991.

IMAGES IN THE EXHIBITION

Salinas Valley Farm, ca. 1938, watercolor, 15 x 21.8 inches

Leon Kirkman Amyx was born in Visalia, California. A 1931 graduate of San Jose State College, he also attended the University of California at Berkeley, California College of Arts and Crafts, and the Claremont Graduate School, from which he received a M.A. degree in 1942. In addition, he studied with Clarence Hinkle, Leon Kroll, Henry Lee McFee and Millard Sheets.

After college Amyx moved to Monterey County, where he began painting scenes of the Salinas Valley, using both watercolor and oil. He exhibited at the Golden Gate International Exposition in 1939, and with the American and National Watercolor Societies during the 1940s. In 1944 Amyx's paintings were included in an exhibition organized by the San Francisco Museum of Art that traveled throughout Latin America.

From 1936 to 1972 Amyx taught painting, design, and the history of art at Hartnell College in Salinas, as well as summer sessions at other institutions including Sacramento State and San Jose State colleges, University of the Pacific, and the Claremont Graduate School.

Amyx was a member of the California Water Color Society, National Watercolor Society and the Carmel Art Association; also an honorary member of the Laguna Beach Art Association and an associate of the American Watercolor Society. He was the recipient of numerous awards.

STANDISH BACKUS, JR. (1910–1989)

Camp by the Sea, 1939 (Monterey), watercolor, 15 x 22.3 inches

A native of Detroit, Michigan, Standish Backus, Jr. began to work in watercolor while studying architecture at Princeton University. He also studied architecture at the University of Munich. Except for a brief period of study with Eliot O'Hara he received no formal art training.

Backus moved to Santa Barbara in 1935, and became acquainted with watercolor painters Hardie Gramatky, Emil Kosa, Barse Miller and Millard Sheets. Beginning in 1938, he exhibited widely in California with, among others, the California Water Color Society, the Los Angeles Museum, and the Oakland Art Gallery. His work was also shown at the 1939 Golden Gate International Exposition and, in 1940, at the Art Institute of Chicago.

During World War II, he served as naval combat artist in the Pacific Theater and in Japan, where his duties included recording the effects of the bombing on Hiroshima. He participated as the official Navy artist in Admiral Richard E. Byrd's 1955 expedition to the South Pole, and in 1967 designed the Pacific War Memorial mosaic mural for Corregidor Island in Manila Bay, Philippines.

Throughout his long career, Backus produced paintings that captured the California scene in an optimistic style typical of the Regionalist movement. He was a member of the American Watercolor Society, the National Watercolor Society, and the American Federation of the Arts.

Night Watchman, 1940, watercolor, 15 x 22 inches

LEE BLAIR (1911–1993)

San Francisco Cable Car Celebration, ca. 1930, watercolor, 15 x 21.5 inches

Lee Everett Blair was born in Los Angeles. From 1931 to 1934 he studied painting at the Chouinard Art Institute, where he began his career as a California scene painter, winning a gold medal in the International Art Competition of the 1932 Olympic Games. While at Chouinard, Blair studied with, among others, Pruett Carter and David Siqueiros. As a student he joined the California Water Color Society and soon began to organize its traveling exhibitions.

After graduation, he and his new wife (and fellow artist) Mary exhibited in the Los Angeles area. During the late 1930s he also worked as a film animator at MGM and Disney Studios, on classic features such as *Pinocchio* and *Fantasia*. Lee taught landscape painting at Chouinard from 1939 to 1942, then served in the Navy's Bureau of Aeronautics.

Lee and Mary Blair moved to New York City in 1946 to run their film production company; while in New York Lee also studied at the Art Students League. In 1968 the Blairs moved back to Northern California, where he taught animation and landscape painting at colleges and universities in the Santa Cruz area.

Blair won many prizes and awards from regional and national organizations, including the California Water Color Society and the American Watercolor Society, from which he received the prestigious Dolphin Fellowship.

MARY BLAIR (1911–1978)

Farm Near Bishop, 1941, watercolor, 18 x 22 inches

Mary Robinson Blair was born in McAlester, Oklahoma and moved to California with her family as a child. After graduating from San Jose State College, she attended the Chouinard Art Institute, where she studied with Pruett Carter and Lawrence Murphy.

Beginning in 1935 Blair began exhibiting regularly with the California Water Color Society, and at various locations in Southern California with her husband, Lee. Beginning in 1936 and continuing through the war she worked as a designer and color director on such animated movies as Disney's *Cinderella* and *Sleeping Beauty.*

Blair moved to New York with her husband in 1946, and began working as a successful freelance commercial artist, illustrat-

ing children's books, and designing magazine covers and Broadway stage sets. She continued her association with Disney, and contributed to several feature films as well as designing attractions for the Disneyland theme park in Anaheim, California. These included *It's a Small World*, which was created as a salute to UNICEF at the 1964 New York World's Fair before being moved to its permanent site at Disneyland, for which Mary also designed murals for *Tomorrowland.*

The Blairs returned to California in 1968. In addition to continuing her watercolor painting, she received a commission to design the ten-story-tall tile mural for a hotel at Disney World in Orlando, Florida.

REX BRANDT, N.A. (1914–2000)

Horsemen at Mission Beach, 1942 (San Diego), egg tempera, 21 x 32 inches

Born in San Diego, Rexford Elson Brandt studied at Riverside Junior College before attending the University of California at Berkeley, where in 1936 he received a B.A. in Fine Arts, followed by postgraduate studies in art education at Stanford. Returning to Southern California, Brandt was made director of the new Riverside Junior College Art Center, a position he retained until 1943.

Thus began a long and varied teaching career that included positions at, among others, Chouinard Art Institute, University of Southern California and Scripps College. During this period Brandt also began exhibiting with the California Water Color Society and became a director of the Works Progress Administration (WPA). In 1937 Brandt assisted Lawson

Cooper to organize *The California Group*, a touring exhibition that developed interest in the California style of watercolor.

In 1947 he and Phil Dike opened the Brandt-Dike Summer School of Painting in Corona Del Mar, where the two artists taught together until 1955; Brandt continued teaching until 1985.

Brandt wrote the first of many influential books on painting in 1949. His honors included awards from the California Water Color Society and the American Watercolor Society (of which he was a Dolphin Fellow), an honorary life member of the National Watercolor Society and a life fellow of the Royal Society of the Arts. He was elected to the National Academy of Design in 1974.

LOIS GREEN COHEN (1919–   )

Bunker Hill Excavation, ca. 1941, watercolor, 21.5 x 30 inches

Lois Green was born and raised in Chicago. She studied at Carnegie Tech in Pittsburgh, then worked for a time as a fashion illustrator in Pittsburgh. In 1938 she moved to Los Angeles, where she continued her studies at the Chouinard Art Institute and at University of California, Los Angeles. During this time Green worked as a motion picture illustrator, painting in her leisure time.

In 1945 she married Eugene Cohen and continued her art career. One of her major undertakings was her paintings for projection at Griffith Observatory, begun in 1973. She also painted a mural for the Harvard University planetarium. She was a member of the California Water Color Society.

TOM CRAIG (1907–1969)

Mill at Ft. Bragg, undated, watercolor, 11.3 x 15.5 inches

A native of Southern California, Thomas Theodore Craig trained as a botanist at Pomona College. However his studies were interrupted when he contracted tuberculosis, forcing him to the desert town of Cathedral City from 1928 to 1932; he graduated in 1934. While living in the desert he began painting and drawing for the first time. After college he attended the Chouinard Art Institute for a short time, studying with F. Tolles Chamberlin, Clarence Hinkle, Millard Sheets and Barse Miller.

Craig taught at Occidental College and the University of Southern California during the 1930s. His work began to be exhibited prominently throughout California, in galleries and museums and with the California Water Color Society, and was included in the 1937 traveling exhibition, *The California*

Group. Craig won a Guggenheim Fellowship in 1941, which gave him the opportunity to travel throughout the Southwest, painting mining towns.

During World War II Craig worked for *Life* magazine as an artist-correspondent in Italy. After 1950 he retired from painting and devoted his time to cultivating and selling hybrid irises in Escondido, California. He became a leading authority on cross-hybridization.

Craig received many awards for his paintings, including prizes from the Oakland Art Gallery and the California Water Color Society.

TOM CRAIG (1907–1969)

Gold Hill, undated, watercolor, 15.6 x 22.3 inches

PHIL DIKE, N.A. (1906–1989)

Philip Latimer Dike was born in Redlands, California. After high school he attended the Chouinard Art Institute and studied with F. Tolles Chamberlin and Clarence Hinkle. In 1928 Dike went to New York to study at the Art Students League.

Returning to Los Angeles the following year, he taught life drawing and landscape painting at Chouinard and had a one-man museum show of his watercolors. During 1930 and 1931 he traveled and painted throughout Europe and exhibited at the Paris Salon in the spring of 1931. Back in Southern California, he returned to teaching at Chouinard, where he remained until 1950.

Dike's work traveled with *The California Group* exhibition in 1937 and was widely exhibited by galleries.

He taught drawing and composition at Walt Disney's training school from 1935 to 1945, and worked as color coordinator and story designer on several animated classics including *Fantasia* and *Snow White*.

In 1947 Dike and Rex Brandt opened the Brandt-Dike Summer School of Painting in Corona Del Mar. In 1950 he was invited by Millard Sheets to join the faculty of Scripps College and the Clare-mont Graduate School, retiring in 1970.

Dike received numerous awards and honors from the California Water Color Society, San Francisco Golden Gate International Exposition, and the American Watercolor Society. In 1953 he was elected to the National Academy of Design.

Harbor Life, 1947, watercolor, 22 x 13 inches

Cathedral City, undated, watercolor, 21 x 28 inches

Smudging, 1930s (Dike Ranch, Redlands, CA), watercolor, 14 x 20 inches

HARDIE GRAMATKY, N.A. (1907–1979)

Hollywood Boulevard, 1930s, watercolor, 15 x 20 inches

Hardie Gramatky was born in Dallas, Texas but grew up in Southern California. He began his career as an artist in 1926 while attending Stanford University. Two years later he moved to Los Angeles, where he studied with Clarence Hinkle, Pruett Carter and R. Tolles Chamberlin at the Chouinard Art Institute and chose watercolor as his primary medium.

Gramatky began exhibiting regularly with the California Water Color Society in 1929. In the 1930s he worked for six years as one of the favorite animators at Walt Disney Studios. He also illustrated for magazines such as *Fortune*, which hired him to cover the disastrous Ohio-Mississippi Valley flood in 1937. Also that year Gramatky's paintings traveled throughout California with *The California Group* exhibition.

Moving to New York in 1936, he worked as a freelance illustrator and began writing and illustrating children's books. Gramatky moved back to Hollywood during World War II to supervise production of training films for the U.S. Army Air Force under the command of Capt. Ronald Reagan. After the war he remained there to work on the production of *G.I. Joe* before returning to New York.

Among the many organizations honoring Gramatky's work were the American Watercolor Society and the 1946 Audubon Artists Exhibition, New York. In 1950 Gramatky was elected a member of the National Academy of Design.

DONG KINGMAN, N.A. (1911–2000)

San Francisco, 1944, watercolor, 20 x 27 inches

Dong Moy Chu Kingman was born in Oakland, California but grew up in Hong Kong after his family moved there during World War I. There he studied Chinese calligraphy and watercolor paintings, and Western-style painting. Kingman moved with his family back to the Bay Area in 1929 and continued his art studies at the Fox & Morgan Art School in Oakland.

Kingman began to paint city scenes. His first one-man show at the San Francisco Art Center in 1936 brought him immediate recognition for his unique style, a blend of Occidental and Oriental traditions. Beginning in 1935 he spent five years working in the watercolor division of the WPA. Kingman was awarded a two-year Guggenheim Fellowship in 1941, which enabled him to travel, study and paint throughout the United States.

After the war Kingman moved to New York where he taught watercolor painting at Columbia University and Hunter College for a number of years. He joined the faculty of the Famous Artists School in Westport, Connecticut in 1954.

During his career Kingman also worked as an illustrator, technical designer for motion picture studios, and on commission for hotels and banks, creating murals and mosaics. His awards include ones from the San Francisco Art Association, Philadelphia Watercolor Club, and the National Academy of Design, to which he was elected in 1951.

EMIL KOSA, JR., N.A. (1903–1968)

San Pedro Harbor, 1930s, watercolor, 13.5 x 19.5 inches

Born in Paris, France, Emil Jean Kosa, Jr. moved to the United States in 1907 when his father, a Czech artist, came here to work. Returning to Europe, Kosa studied at the Prague Academy of Fine Arts and Charles University in Prague, from which he graduated in 1921. He came to Los Angeles and enrolled at the California Art Institute in 1922 while assisting his father in the mural decoration of churches, public buildings and homes. In 1927 he won a scholarship to Paris' *Ecole des Beaux-Arts*, where he studied through 1928.

Back in Los Angeles in 1928, he met Millard Sheets and studied for a time at the Chouinard Art Institute. From 1933 to 1968 Kosa worked as a special effects artist for Twentieth

Century Fox, winning a 1963 Academy Award for his work on the movie *Cleopatra*. He had solo exhibits yearly throughout Southern California and occasionally in the East. During this period he also taught at Chouinard and the Laguna Beach School of Art.

Kosa worked at Twentieth-Century Fox for thirty-five years. In his spare time he painted and helped to create the "California style" of watercolor painting. He was an active member of the California Water Color Society. Other honors and awards include recognitions from the 1928 Panama Pacific Exposition, American Watercolor Society. He was elected to the National Academy of Design in 1951.

Chavez Ravine, 1932, watercolor, 15 x 19.3 inches

DAN LUTZ (1906–1978)

Steam Shovel, 1937, watercolor, 13.3 x 19.8 inches

Dan Lutz was born in Decatur, Illinois and studied briefly at Milliken University before enrolling at the Art Institute of Chicago, where he studied from 1928 to 1931. In 1931 the Art Institute awarded Lutz a traveling fellowship, which enabled him to study in Europe for a year.

On his return, Lutz moved to Los Angeles and joined the fine arts faculty at the University of Southern California, completing work for his B.F.A. degree at the same time. He remained at USC until 1942, and was named head of the painting department in 1938. Lutz taught at the Chouinard Art Institute from 1944 to 1952 and in summer sessions both at the Art Institute of Chicago and in Michigan.

After 1936 he exhibited regularly with the California Water Color Society as well as Southern California galleries and museums. In the early 1940s, inspired by Negro spirituals, Lutz began a series of expressionistic oil paintings, which received notable distinction. A serious amateur musician, he also developed a series of paintings based on various musical themes. In the 1950s and 1960s he continued to paint regularly, lectured occasionally, and traveled widely.

Among Lutz's many honors were awards by the National Academy of Design; the National Watercolor Exhibition, Pennsylvania Academy; and the California Water Color Society.

Fruit Stand, 1934 (Hoover and 24th Streets, Los Angeles), oil, 21.3 x 25.3 inches

BARSE MILLER, N.A. (1904–1973)

Auburn, California, ca. 1945, watercolor, 14.5 x 21.8 inches

A native of New York City, Barse Miller came from a family of noted artists, including inventor and painter Samuel F.B. Morse. He attended the National Academy of Design and the Pennsylvania Academy of Fine Arts. While studying at the latter he was awarded two traveling scholarships, which allowed him to study in Paris. Miller moved to Los Angeles in 1924 and began teaching at the Chouinard Art Institute in 1927. He also taught for many years at the Art Center School in Los Angeles, and in the 1930s directed its summer school in Newport Beach. During the Depression he was a mural artist for the WPA. Miller taught with Rex Brandt and Paul Sample at the University of Vermont in the summer of 1940.

Over the years Miller had numerous one-man shows in galleries and museums in both New York and Los Angeles. Influenced by the work of Jose Clemente Orozco, he designed and executed a number of major murals, including several commissioned by the WPA. His work was included in the 1937 exhibition, *The California Group*.

In 1941 Miller was a special correspondent for *Life* magazine, documenting the training of troops at Fort Ord, California. During the war he served overseas as chief of the Combat Art Section for the Pacific Theater. After the war he received a Guggenheim Fellowship and moved to New York where he taught briefly at the Art Students League before becoming a professor and, later, department chairman at Queens College. He also formed and operated a summer school in watercolor painting in Maine. He returned occasionally to California to give private lessons and also taught at the Rex Brandt Summer School in 1966.

In addition to his election to the National Academy of Design in 1947, Miller's many honors were awards from the Pennsylvania Academy of Fine Arts; the Los Angeles Museum of History, Science and Art; California Art Club and the California Water Color Society.

Rainy Day – Fort Mason, 1943, watercolor, 15 x 22 inches

Phil Paradise, N.A. (1905–1997)

Phillip Herschel Paradise was born in Oregon but grew up in Bakersfield, California. He studied at the Santa Barbara School of the Arts with Frank Morley Fletcher and at the Chouinard Art Institute with F. Tolles Chamberlin and Pruett Carter from 1927 to 1931. Later he studied with Leon Kroll, Rico Lebrun, and David Siqueiros.

After graduating from Chouinard in 1931 Paradise began teaching there, and was its director of fine arts from 1936 to 1940. He was an art director and production designer at Paramount Studios until 1948, and worked as a commercial artist for several magazines from 1940 to 1960. During this period he actively exhibited his watercolors in galleries in Los Angeles and New York.

Paradise joined, and began exhibiting with, the California Water Color Society in the late 1920s. His early work concentrated on regional scenes of the Los Angeles area. During the 1940s the focus of his work shifted to subject matter gleaned from travels to Mexico, Central America and the Caribbean, and his technique became more stylized.

Paradise lectured at the University of Texas, El Paso, and taught at Scripps College, substituting for Millard Sheets. In the 1940s he established a workshop in printmaking in Cambria, California, and later directed the Cambria Summer School. The recipient of many awards and honors, Paradise was elected to the National Academy of Design in 1994.

Delivery at Headquarters, 1942, watercolor and gouache, 12 x 18 inches

Evening on the Homefront, 1942, watercolor, 17 x 23 inches

The Morning After, 1942, watercolor and gouache, 14 x 22 inches

Messengers of Mercy, 1942, watercolor, 16 x 22 inches

In early 1942 the Red Cross sent out artists fliers asking for war & disaster relief paintings they might use in a traveling show to arouse interest in their projects. I was intrigued & challenged. First I made a list, selected the most challenging subjects, and painted the four, hoping that at least one would be considered worthy. The Red Cross chose all four, used them in more than one show during the war years. To my surprise all were returned to me at war's end, with a "thank you" letter....

I did almost no research for the works; they were already part of my background experience: the 1933 Long Beach-Torrance-Watts earthquake.... Radio [reports] sent us to the disaster. The rest was routine with my life style of that period.

[From a 1993 letter from Phil Paradise to the Martins]

DOUGLASS PARSHALL, N.A. (1899–1990)

Gypsies, 1940s, watercolor, 16 x 22 inches

Born in New York City, Douglass Ewell Parshall was the son of noted landscape artist DeWitt Parshall. He began painting under his father's guidance as a child, and was given his first art exhibition at age ten at a well-known New York gallery. He attended the Art Students League in New York. In 1917 the family moved to Santa Barbara, where young Parshall attended Thacher School in Ojai before continuing his studies at the Santa Barbara School of the Arts with Frank Morley Fletcher.

During the Depression Parshall was a district supervisor of the Federal Arts Project. He was known for his society portraits in the 1920s and 1930s, but later focused on landscapes and allegorical studies. In the 1950s and 1960s he developed a more impressionistic style and was concerned with bright color and motion.

Parshall traveled extensively throughout the world. He was also one of the founders of the Santa Barbara Art Institute, where he taught from 1967 to 1975, and was a founding member of the Santa Barbara Art Association. Early in his career Parshall began receiving awards for his work, including major prizes from the California Water Color Society and the National Academy of Design, to which he was elected in 1969.

James Patrick (1911–1944)

Railroad Trestle at Elk, undated, watercolor, 15 x 22.6 inches

James Hollins Patrick was born in British Columbia and came to California with his family as an infant. He attended high school in Hollywood after they moved to Los Angeles County, and then attended the Chouinard Art Institute on a three-year scholarship.

Completing his studies, Patrick taught figure drawing and landscape painting at Chouinard for three years, to which he returned in 1937. He continued to teach there until 1942, and often took students to various locations in the Los Angeles area to create spontaneous watercolors of city scenes. In 1935 he became a member of the California Water Color Society. During this period he assisted Millard Sheets on several major mural commissions, and worked as a pre-production artist for Columbia, Universal and United Artists studios.

In 1942 the Los Angeles Museum of History, Science and Art had a one-man show of his oils and watercolors. Two years later, at the age of thirty-three, he died of pulmonary tuberculosis.

CHARLES PAYZANT (1898–1980)

The Ball Players, 1939, watercolor, 14.5 x 22 inches

Charles St. George Payzant was born and raised in Nova Scotia. After service in World War I he studied in Canada and England before moving to Los Angeles in the 1920s. Once in Southern California he studied at the Otis Art Institute and then at the Chouinard Art Institute.

Throughout the 1930s and 1940s, Payzant worked as a freelance commercial artist and, for twelve years, as an artist at Walt Disney Studios, where he produced backgrounds for such classic films as *Fantasia* and *Pinocchio*. He continued to produce many fine watercolors and illustrated children's books that were written by his wife, Terry. He also served as art director for the "Dick and Jane" educational series for Mac Millan Publishing Company, and produced several murals on private commission.

Payzant exhibited sporadically with the California Water Color Society beginning in 1930. In 1931 he was awarded first prize for painting in the annual exhibition at the Los Angeles Museum of History, Science and Art.

Early Wilshire Boulevard, 1931, watercolor, 11.5 x 15 inches

GEORGE POST (1906–1997)

San Francisco Waterfront, Ships Tied at Waterfront, 1936, watercolor, 17 x 23 inches. WPA Federal Art Project Series 696

George Booth Post was born and raised in the San Francisco Bay Area, and attended the California School of Fine Arts (now the San Francisco Art Institute). After completing his studies in 1927 he worked in a variety of fields from advertising to printing. During this period he developed an interest in watercolor painting and was essentially self-taught in that medium.

For a time during the Depression Post lived in the Mother Lode country of California. While there he painted a mural, *Lumbering, Mining, and Agriculture*, for Sonora High School as a WPA project. From 1937 to 1938, he traveled and painted in Mexico and Europe.

Post's teaching career began in 1940, first as an instructor at Stanford University and then, from 1947 to 1973, as a professor of fine arts at the California College of Arts and Crafts in Oakland. During the summers of 1945 and 1955 Post taught at the Brandt-Dike Summer School of Painting in Corona del Mar, and then at the Rex Brandt Summer School until 1977. He also instructed at San Jose State College and the San Diego Fine Arts Gallery.

He exhibited with, and won several awards from, the California Water Color Society. Post's work also received recognition from the Art Institute of Chicago; the Springfield, Missouri Art Museum and the Society of Western Artists.

EDWARD REEP (1918–)

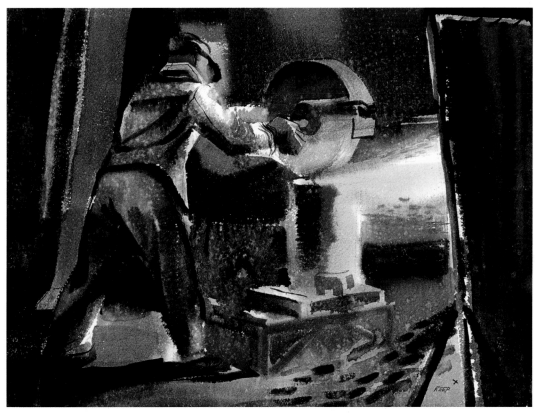

Grinder, 1939, watercolor, 14 x 21 inches

Edward Arnold Reep was born in Brooklyn, New York and raised in Southern California, where he studied with Barse Miller at the Art Center School in Los Angeles from 1936 to 1942. He began exhibiting with the California Water Color Society while still a student.

In 1941 Reep was commissioned by the government to complete a mural at Fort Ord, California. Enlisting in the Army at the beginning of World War II, he was an official war artist for the North African and Italian campaigns. Frequently under fire, he was awarded the Bronze Star, received two battlefield promotions and left the Army as a Captain.

Awarded a Guggenheim Fellowship upon his discharge in 1947, Reep returned to Los Angeles to teach painting and

drawing at the Art Center School until 1950. He also taught at the Chouinard Art Institute until 1969, by then renamed the California Institute of the Arts. He was appointed chairman of the department of painting in 1957. He became professor and artist-in-residence at East Carolina University in Greenville, North Carolina, in 1970.

Reep was a scenic artist for the motion picture industry, and also received painting commissions from *Life* magazine and the Ford Motor Company. Author of a 1969 book on watercolor painting, Reep's awards include a prize from the Los Angeles County Museum and a National Endowment for the Arts grant.

HERBERT RYMAN (1910–1989)

MGM Marina *(Boats on Backlot), ca. 1950, watercolor, 14 x 19.5 inches*

Herbert Dickens Ryman was born in Vernon, Illinois. He attended Millikin University in Decatur, Illinois before enrolling in the school of the Art Institute of Chicago, from which he graduated Magna Cum Laude.

Moving to Southern California in 1932, he settled in Hollywood where he spent fifty years as an artist in the movie industry, including some years as the sole artist and illustrator for MGM Studios. From 1938 to 1941, he was also an instructor at the Chouinard Art Institute, and during World War II he produced indoctrination films for the U.S. government. In 1939 he joined Walt Disney, working as an illustrator and sometimes art director on such films as *Fantasia*, *Dumbo* and *Pinocchio*. He also worked on design concepts for Disneyland and Walt Disney World in Florida, and created the first large panoramic maps of Disneyland and other Disney theme parks. Ryman's work also involved projects for the Ringling Brother's Circus, when he did a number of portraits of clowns, including Emmett Kelly.

Ryman was president of the California Art Club, Fellow of the American Institute of Fine Arts, and a member of the Society of Illustrators and many other organizations.

MILLARD SHEETS, N.A. (1907–1989)

New Arrivals, undated, watercolor, 21.5 x 29.3 inches

Millard Owen Sheets was born in Pomona, California and grew up on a ranch east of Los Angeles. After high school he studied at the Chouinard Art Institute with Clarence Hinkle and F. Tolles Chamberlin. After graduating he spent several months traveling and painting in Central America, South America and Europe.

Returning to Los Angeles in 1930, he began teaching at Chouinard before accepting a position at Scripps College, where he taught from 1936 to 1955. Sheets joined the California Water Color Society in 1927; his work was included in *The California Group* exhibition in 1937.

From 1933 to 1935 Sheets served as a regional director for the Southern California Public Works of Art Program. During World War II he was an artist-correspondent for *Life* magazine in the China-Burma-India Theater.

Sheets also had an impressive career as an architectural designer and muralist. Before the war he designed seventeen training schools for the Army Air Corps and, from 1954 to 1975, designed many buildings throughout California. Sheets was director of Otis Art Institute in Los Angeles from 1953 to 1959.

Sheets' prizes and awards include honors from the Los Angeles Museum, Art Institute of Chicago and Pennsylvania Academy of Fine Arts. He also received honorary degrees from Otis Art Institute and Notre Dame University. He was a Dolphin Fellow of the American Watercolor Society and was elected to the National Academy of Design in 1947.

OSCAR VAN YOUNG (1906–1991)

Industrial Neighborhood, City of the Angels, 1946, oil, 24.3 x 28 inches

Oscar Van Young was born and raised in Vienna, Austria. In 1919 he received a scholarship to study art at the Art Academy in Odessa, Russia, but after several years of instruction, fled the country because of political unrest. After traveling around Europe he immigrated to the United States and settled in Chicago, where he continued his art education at the Academy of Fine Arts and began to exhibit his works. In 1940 he moved to Los Angeles and studied at California State University, Los Angeles.

His watercolor paintings from this era often depicted run-down buildings, street scenes, and other city subjects. Most of these representational paintings were done in a painterly style, with opaque colors, and completed while on location.

Van Young exhibited with the California Water Color Society. He also had a one-man show at the Los Angeles County Museum in 1942. Throughout the 1950s he continued to paint and exhibit his watercolors nationally. He gradually became interested in working in a more abstract style and, beginning in the 1960s, painted almost exclusively with oils on canvas.

Van Young was an art instructor at the Otis Art Institute and various universities. He also worked as a print maker, producing limited edition fine art lithographs.

JOSEPH WEISMAN (1907–1994)

Purple Duck Café, 1939 (Los Angeles), watercolor, 17 x 22 inches

Born in Schenectady, New York Joseph Weisman grew up in Cleveland. Because of his mother's ill health, his family moved to Los Angeles in the 1920s. After graduating from high school, Weisman received a scholarship to attend the Chouinard Art Institute, where he studied with Clarence Hinkle and Millard Sheets from 1925 to 1929. He later studied at the Art Center School in Los Angeles with Barse Miller.

During World War II, he was a technical illustrator for Douglas Aircraft Corporation, then from 1946 to 1949 he worked in the scenic art departments of MGM, Twentieth-Century Fox and Warner Brothers studios.

Throughout his career he exhibited with such groups as the California Water Color Society, which he had joined in the 1930s; the San Diego Fine Arts Society; the Oakland Art Gallery and the Los Angeles Museum of History, Science and Art. His work was also included in exhibitions at the Dayton Art Institute and the Pennsylvania Academy of Fine Arts.

Weisman was especially interested in the unique architecture and people in the old Chinatown district of Los Angeles. After World War II he expanded his repertoire to include Southwest landscapes and portraits.

Beginning in the 1950s, Weisman worked primarily as a teacher, both with the Los Angeles City Adult School System and privately.

First House on Olvera Street, 1929 (Los Angeles), watercolor, 10 x 13 inches

Old Los Angeles Mule Market, 1930, watercolor, 11 x 14.5 inches

JOSEPH WEISMAN (1907–1994)

Early Morn', Chinatown, 1947 (Los Angeles), oil, 22 x 26 inches

RAY WILSON (1906–1972)

Fishing, San Francisco Bay, 1930s, watercolor, 14 x 21 inches

Raymond Clifford Wilson was born in Oakland, California but spent his childhood in Baltimore. He moved back to Oakland in 1921.

During the early years of the Depression, he worked as a shipping clerk and as a longshoreman. Following study at the College of Arts and Crafts in Oakland, Wilson was crippled in a swimming accident in the early 1930s. While recuperating he began to paint watercolors of the Bay Area. These were well received, but he suffered a mental breakdown in 1940 and spent the rest of his life in mental institutions.

Wilson's tragically short career was distinguished. His work was shown in the late 1930s in a national traveling exhibition organized by the Art Institute of Chicago, at the San Francisco Museum of Art, the California Palace of the Legion of Honor, and at the 1939-40 Golden Gate International Exposition.

MILFORD ZORNES, N.A. (1908–2008)

Cerro Romualdo, 1937, (San Luis Obispo), watercolor, 22 x 30.5 inches

James Milford Zornes was born in Oklahoma and lived in Boise, Idaho before moving to Los Angeles in 1925. Following a brief career in the U.S. Merchant Marine, his formal education included studies at Pomona College and Otis Art Institute, with F. Tolles Chamberlin and Millard Sheets.

Zornes worked for the Federal Art Project in 1933, producing both paintings and murals in public buildings. He taught at Otis Art Institute from 1938 to 1942, then during World War II served as an Army artist in the China-Burma-India Theater. After the war he worked in Chicago on a mural project with Maynard Dixon before returning to California.

Beginning in 1946 Zornes taught at a number of institutions, including Pomona College, the Pasadena School of Fine Arts,

University of California, Santa Barbara and the Rex Brandt Summer School. He also taught summer classes in Mount Carmel, Utah. In addition to his work as a painter, Zornes was a freelance writer, cartoonist and surveyor for the General Land Office in Yellowstone National Park.

Zornes was active in the California Water Color Society from 1934 on, and his work was included in the 1937 traveling exhibition, *The California Group*. In addition to his election as a member of the National Academy of Design in 1994, his honors included awards from the Chicago International Watercolor Exhibition, Art Institute of Chicago and the American Watercolor Society.

THIS EXHIBITION IS MADE POSSIBLE
THROUGH THE GENEROUS SUPPORT OF:

Anonymous
Louise Clarke & John Carbon
Astrid & Lawrence T. Hammett
Marlene & Warren Miller
Eleanor Van Cott

Exhibition Guest Curator: Marlene R. Miller
Catalogue Design: Garcin Media Group
Editors: Warren Miller and Michael Redmon

Printing and Binding: Haagen Printing Co., Santa Barbara, CA